Leaves! Leaves! Leaves!

Leaves! Leaves! Leaves!

Written and Illustrated by
Nancy Elizabeth Wallace

SCHOLASTIC INC.
New York   Toronto   London   Auckland   Sydney
Mexico City   New Delhi   Hong Kong   Buenos Aires

Artist's Pencil

midnight black

Artist's Pencil

forest green

Artist's Pencil

robin's egg blue

ISBN 0-439-67928-1

12 11 10 9 8 7 6 5 4 3 2 1   4 5 6 7 8 9/0

Printed in the U.S.A.   40

First Scholastic printing, September 2004

Book design by Virginia Pope

The text for this book is set in 16-point Bernhard Gothic.

The illustrations are rendered in cut paper, crayons, and colored pencils.

For all of the seasons of our lives—with love

To Pat, Helen, Maryrose,
Linda J, Peggy, Sue D.,
Danna and Kathy;
Rhea and Keat,
Diane and Harvee,
Emmy and Ken,
John and Robin,
Deb and Jay

Special thanks to
Margery and Anahid,
and always for my best buddy, Peter

magnifying glass

ZIP-IT BAG

Artist's Pencil — buttercup yellow

Artist's Pencil — dirt brown

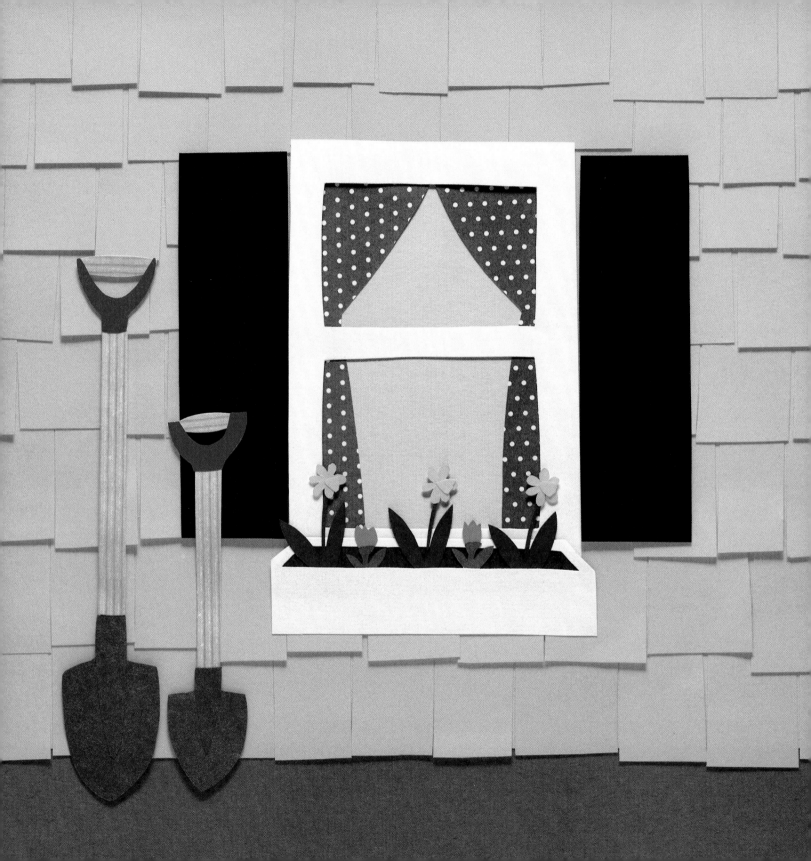

Spring

"It's spring!" said Mama. "Would you like to go on a leaf walk, Buddy Bear?"

"Yes," said Buddy. "I like to find leaves."

The early spring air felt warm.
The earth was cool and damp.
"Where are the leaves, Mama?"
asked Buddy.

Mama tugged gently on a branch.
"Look carefully.
What do you see?"
"I see bumps."
"Those are buds,"
said Mama.
Buddy touched
a bud.

"The new leaves are folded up very tightly inside.
     The bud scales protect the leaves. When the bud scales open, the young leaves will start to unfold."

"Like this?" asked Buddy.

"Yes, my little Bud."
They walked farther on.
The sun felt warm and nice.

Buddy picked a leaf.
"What do you see?"
Mama asked.

"I see this flat part."
"That's the blade."
"I see lines."
"Those are the veins."
"The part I'm holding
is the stem," said Buddy.

"How do leaves know when it's time to come out, Mama?"

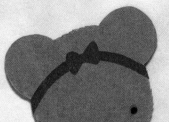

"It's spring. The daylight hours are growing longer. The spring rain has been falling. The weather is getting warmer. It's time for the leaves to come out and start making food for the trees," she answered.

"*Food!* I'm hungry too," said Buddy. "Let's eat!"

They ate crackers and drank juice.

"Mama, what did the big leaf say to the little leaf?"
"What?"
"Don't *leave* me."
Mama laughed.

Summer

"It's summer!" said Mama. "Would you like to go on another leaf walk, Buddy Bear?"

"Yes!" said Buddy.

"I want to find

lots of leaves."

COOL IT!

Artist's Pencils

8 colors

The summer air felt hot.
Mama and Buddy put down their blanket at the edge of the woods.
"Mama, go look for some leaves. I'll look for some too," said Buddy.

Artist's Pencils

8 colors

Drawing Pad

COOL IT!

First they spread Buddy's leaves on the blanket.

"What do you see?" asked Mama.

"I see shapes!" said Buddy. "One looks like a star. I see one that looks like a heart. There's kind of a round one, and a skinny one that looks like a feather. One leaf looks like a mitten, and one looks like a fan."

"Leaves have different edges too, Buddy," said Mama. "Look at mine. Do you see a leaf that's jagged? And one that has an edge like a saw?"

"Yes," said Buddy. "And I see a wavy one and one that's smooth."

"I'm still looking," said Buddy. "All of the leaves have something the same."
"What's that, Buddy?"

"They're all green! Why, Mama?"
"They're green because of chlorophyll."
"Klor-o-fil? What's that?" asked Buddy.

Mama started to draw a picture on Buddy's drawing pad.
She explained, "It's a chemical that's in the leaves in spring and in summer."

"Chlorophyll helps the leaves turn the sunlight and the rain and part of the air and nutrients from the soil into food for the plant."

"How?" asked Buddy.

"When we breathe, we breathe out a gas called carbon dioxide. The tree takes this gas in through teeny tiny openings in its leaves."

Buddy breathed into his paw. He looked. "I don't see any carbon dioxide." "You're right," said Mama. "It's invisible."

Mama kept drawing.
Buddy helped.
"Rain water and
nutrients travel
from the earth
into the roots,
up the trunk,
through the branches,
through the stems
and into the leaves."

"The sun shines on the leaves. The chlorophyll in the leaves, and the water and nutrients that come from the earth, and the carbon dioxide that comes from the air make the food that travels to all parts of the tree."

Artist's Pencils
8 colors

COOL IT!

"The leaves are making *food*. I'm hungry," said Buddy. "Let's eat."

They ate berries and drank lemonade.

"I'm a leaf, Mama. I'm sucking the water and nutrients up, up, up . . . *ssssssss*. Mama?"

"Yes, Buddy."

"What did the tree take on vacation?"

"What?"

"A trunk!"

Buddy laughed.

Fall

"It's fall!" said Mama. "Would you like to take another walk and collect leaves, Buddy Bear?"

"I like collecting leaves," said Buddy.

Ozzie's Orchard

ZIP-IT BAG

The air was cool and crisp.
The leaves crunched under their feet.
Buddy yelled, "Red . . . orange . . . yellow . . . Leaves!"

"Why did the leaves change, Mama?"

"In the fall there are fewer daylight hours, so there is less sunlight. The ground and air are colder. The chlorophyll that made the leaves green is disappearing. The yellow and orange that have been there all the time can now be seen."

"What about red?" asked Buddy.

"The red is made from leftover food in the leaves," explained Mama.

"Hold my hands, Buddy Bear," said Mama. "I am the tree, you are the leaf. When the leaves are new and young, they are connected to the tree. In spring . . . in summer . . . in the wind . . . in the rain. By fall the leaves are old. They have done their job."

"Now, Leaf, hold on by one finger. What will happen, Leaf, when it rains, when the wind blows?"

"I'll fallllllll!" shouted Buddy. "I think that's why this season is called fall, Mama. I'm hungry. Let's eat!"

They sat on a rock and ate apples and drank apple juice.
"Mama?"
"Yes, Buddy."

"What has bark but no bite?"
"What?"
"A tree!"
Mama giggled.

Winter

"It's winter," said Mama Bear.
"Let's go for a leaf walk," shouted Buddy.

The winter air was cold and dry.
The earth was covered with snow.
High up in a tree a few pale brown
leaves still held on. They rustled in the wind.
"The leaves are almost gone, Mama!"

"The trees are resting," said Mama. "In their roots, food is stored for winter. The leaves that fell in the fall are under the snow."

Buddy found a leaf.
"Look, Mama. This leaf has brown veins and lots of holes."
"Yes, Buddy. The leaves are rotting. The food that's left in them is changing into rich earth that will feed the trees and plants through their roots."

Mama pulled gently on a branch.
"What do you see?"
"Buds!" shouted Buddy.
"Yes, my winter Buddy. They're waiting
for spring.

It's getting cold. Let's go inside."
"I'm getting hungry," said Buddy. "Let's go eat!"

Mama and Buddy ate some soup.
"Mama?"
"Yes, Buddy."

"What did the tree say to the bear cub in winter?"
"What?"
"I'm bare, you're Bear!"
Mama chuckled.

Then, while the trees rested, Mama and Buddy rested too.

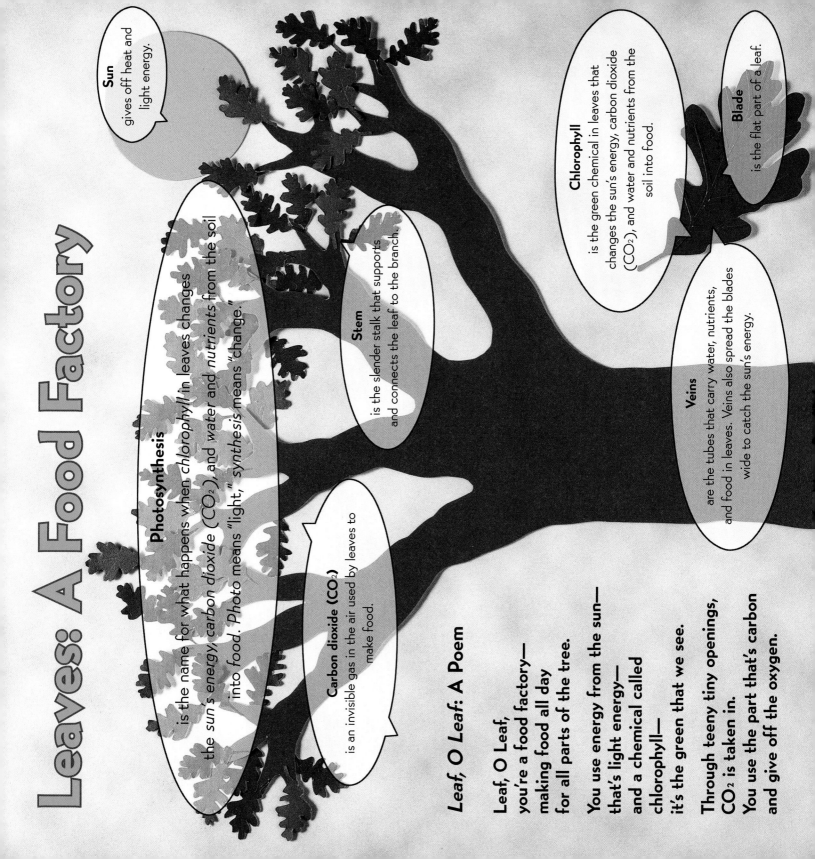

Trunk, the tree's main stem. Water and nutrients travel up from the soil to the branches and the leaves. Food made by the leaves is carried through the trunk to all parts of the tree to be used or stored.

Nutrients come from rotted leaves, which make soil rich and fertile.

Roots are the part of a tree that is underground. Water and nutrients in the soil travel into the roots, up the trunk, and into the leaves to make food. Food is also stored in the roots.

Water in the soil comes from rain, snow, sleet, hail, and fog.

There's water in the soil; there are nutrients too. In the roots and up the trunk, they travel up to you.

Nutrients, water, CO₂, sunlight! This is what you use, Leaf. The recipe is right.

You put it all together; you're a food factory. The sugar that you make feeds all parts of the tree.

WOW!

Rub-a-Leaf

In the fall take a leaf walk and gather different kinds of leaves.

Art Activity . . . Art Activity . . . Art Activity

1. Place a single layer of leaves between two paper towels on a flat surface.

2. Put a plastic bag on top.

3. Pile heavy books on your paper towel "sandwich."

4. Let the leaves flatten and dry for several days.

5. When the leaves are dry, place them under a piece of thin paper on a flat surface.

6. Rub a dark-colored crayon over the paper. The shapes of the leaves, the stems, and the veins will appear.

7. Cut out the leaf rubbings.

8. Arrange them on colored paper.

9. You can label the kinds of leaves, add leaf jokes such as the ones in this book, or write a leaf poem.

Sassafras Leaves

On one branch,
I can count three
different shaped leaves
on a sassafras tree!

Tulip Poplar

Scarlet Oak

White Oak

Ginkgo

Eastern Redbud

Sweet gum

Maple

Sassafras

Serviceberry

Dogwood

Willow

Sassafras

Birch

Elm